## The Technology of Farming

# Producing Grains

Barbara A. Somervill

Chicago, Illinois

8/14          CS          24.49

**www.capstonepub.com**
Visit our website to find out
more information about
Heinemann-Raintree books.

**To order:**

☎ Phone 888-454-2279

▣ Visit www.capstonepub.com
to browse our catalog and order online.

Edited by Abby Colich, Megan Cotugno, and Nancy Dickmann
Designed by Victoria Allen
Picture research by Elizabeth Alexander
Illustrations by Geoff Ward

Originated by Capstone Global Library Ltd
Printed and bound in China by China Translation and Printing
Services Ltd

16 15 14 13 12
10 9 8 7 6 5 4 3 2 1

**Library of Congress Cataloging-in-Publication Data**
Somervill, Barbara A.
  Producing grains / Barbara A. Somervill.—1st ed.
     p. cm.—(The technology of farming)
  Includes bibliographical references and index.
  ISBN 978-1-4329-6409-2 (hb)—ISBN 978-1-4329-6416-0 (pb)
1. Grain—Juvenile literature. 2. Grain trade—Juvenile literature.
I. Title. II. Series: Technology of farming.
  SB189.S57 2012
  664.7—dc23                      2011037568

**Acknowledgments**
We would like to thank the following for permission to
reproduce photographs: Alamy: p. 6 (© Doug Peebles
Photography); Corbis: pp. 7 (© Earl & Nazima Kowall), 12 (Frank
Conlon); Getty Images: pp. 8 (Dagli Orti), 9 (Frederic J. Brown/
AFP), 11 (The Bridgeman Art Library), 35 (Bloomberg/ Patrick
Fallon), 37 (AFP/ William West); Photolibrary: pp. 28, 33 (Still
Pictures/Adrian Arbib), 34; © Sarah Montgomery/The Garden's
Edge: p. 23; Shutterstock: pp. 5 (© Bernabea Amalia Mendez),
14 (© frog-traveller), 15 (© Fidel), 17 (© Heike Rau), 18 (© Robyn
Mackenzie), 19 (© Frontpage), 20 (© Ildi Papp), 24 (© takayuki),
26 (© bogdan ionescu), 29 (© Kletr), 30 (© Mosista Pambudi),
31 (© Monkey Business Images), 42 (© Fishking), 43 (© Elena
Elisseeva).

Cover photo of a combine harvesting wheat reproduced with
permission from Shutterstock (© Kletr).

Every effort has been made to contact copyright holders of
any material reproduced in this book. Any omissions will
be rectified in subsequent printings if notice is given to the
publisher.

**Disclaimer**
All the Internet addresses (URLs) given in this book were valid
at the time of going to press. However, due to the dynamic
nature of the Internet, some addresses may have changed, or
sites may have changed or ceased to exist since publication.
While the author and publisher regret any inconvenience this
may cause readers, no responsibility for any such changes can
be accepted by either the author or the publisher.

# Contents

Some words appear in the text in bold, **like this**. You can find out what they mean by looking in the glossary.

# Who Eats Grain?

The basic food of a person's diet is called a **staple**. Every culture has a staple food, and most staples are grains. The most common staples are rice, wheat, corn, and oats. We eat grains in bread and cereal. Grain can be a side dish, such as fried rice, or the main course, as with pasta. Grain is the main ingredient in pancakes, French crepes, and Mexican tortillas.

Rice is a staple eaten three times a day in countries such as Japan. The Japanese eat *asagohan*, or "steamed morning rice," for breakfast. Add soybean paste, seaweed, grilled fish, or rolled omelet, and you have a full meal. Japanese boxed lunches, called *bento*, contain rice, fish, vegetables, and fruit. In the evening chicken or fish and vegetables are stir-fried and served with rice.

## Wheat

One of the most popular grains worldwide is wheat. Wheat arrives on our tables in loaves of bread, pita, matzo, rolls, muffins, and noodles. Even bread takes many forms. Bread can be thick, fluffy loaves of white bread, dense whole-wheat bread, round flatbreads, or long, crusty baguettes of French bread.

Wheat can be the main ingredient in a meal, such as in pizza or lasagna. Wheat can be part of a side dish, such as macaroni and cheese or couscous. Cracked wheat goes well with parsley and mint in tabbouleh, a Lebanese salad. Wheat is also used for making desserts, including cakes, pies, tarts, and puddings.

Whole-grain bread provides energy. fiber. and protein.

## A tradition of corn

Grinding corn by hand and making tortillas on a skillet is an ancient tradition in Central and South America. The basic ingredients for tortillas are simple: cornmeal and water. In the same way that rice is the staple of Chinese and Japanese diets, corn is the staple food in Mexico, Peru, Ecuador, and many Central American countries. Corn tortillas are on the table for breakfast, lunch, and dinner.

Corn has been eaten in Latin America for more than 9,500 years. Today it is eaten fresh as grilled corn on the cob. It is shaved off the cobs and cooked with zucchini or chilies. Corn is dried and ground into cornmeal for tortillas and cornbread.

Many women still make tortillas by hand the same way their grandmothers did.

Ethiopians share their food off a bread platter called *injera*. This photo shows how it's made.

## Breaking bread

Not all cultures have wheat, rice, or corn. Some people eat different staple grains, such as millet, kamut, oats, or teff. Teff is the main grain of Ethiopia. It is used to make *injera*, which is the bread, the platter, and the eating utensil of Ethiopian dinners. It is a round, flat bread about the size of a large pizza that is placed on a small tabletop. Helpings of stew and vegetable dishes are spooned onto the *injera*. Diners tear off a small piece of *injera* and scoop up the food. Eat the *injera* and a bit of stew in one or two bites. Then tear off another bit of this uniquely Ethiopian bread and try another dish.

# When Did People Start Farming Grain?

The first grains grew wild throughout the world. **Hunter-gatherer clans** collected nuts, berries, and grains. Clans followed large game animals. When clans had hunted until there were no more large game animals available, they had to find other food sources. They gathered seeds from wild grain, such as wheat or barley. People began to clear land and plant the seeds they collected. The seeds produced the first grain crops.

People began planting their own wheat as early as 10,000 BCE in Syria, Jordan, and Turkey. People dried wheat berries and ground them to make flatbread. They began keeping farm animals and fed them leftover wheat straw. Some people wove the straw into sleeping mats, baskets, and **thatch** for roofs. By 5000 BCE wheat farming had spread to Egypt's Nile River area. The Egyptians used wheat to make flour and alcohol.

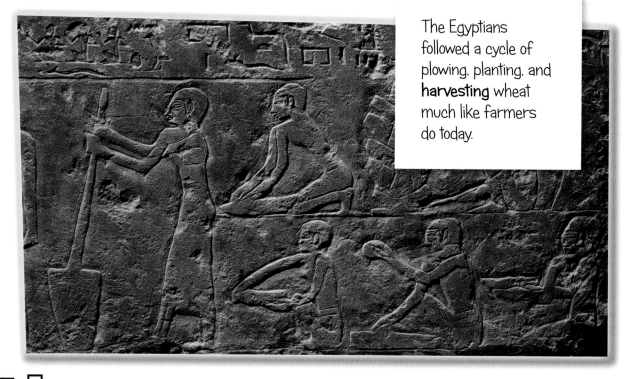

The Egyptians followed a cycle of plowing, planting, and **harvesting** wheat much like farmers do today.

Rice paddies need large amounts of standing water.

## History of other grains

In the Americas, hunter-gatherers in present-day Mexico ate teosinte, an early type of corn, as early as 7500 BCE. Corn became North America's first grain crop. By 1000 CE American Indians across the continent planted corn, beans, and squash in the same fields. Called the "Three Sisters," these crops fed native people throughout the year.

Rice farming began on the other side of the world. In roughly 2000 BCE, southern China's wetlands yielded crops of wild rice. The planting and eating of rice spread westward along trade routes. Arabs brought rice planting to Spain in the 900s CE. By the 15th century, Italy, France, and Spain grew rice.

Growing grains became the foundation of **agriculture**. People saved some of the grain from the previous year for planting the following year. The type of grain grown depended on the **climate** and the soil. A new profession was born—the farmer.

## Slow advances in technology

Over several thousand years, the tools used to grow grains slowly developed. Hand **plows** gave way to larger wooden plows pulled by horses or oxen. In Europe farmers continued to use iron-tipped wooden plows until the 1700s, when Joseph Foljambe developed the first usable iron plow. Stronger iron plows allowed farmers to prepare more land for crops. Wheat, rye, barley, and oat crops increased.

Planting seed was backbreaking work. Planters used small sticks to poke holes in the soil, dropped in a seed or two, and covered up the soil. In 1701 British farmer Jethro Tull (see box) developed a horse-drawn seed drill. The seed drill made planting more efficient.

### Jethro Tull
### (1674–1741)

Jethro Tull farmed wheat in Berkshire, England. Tull saw the need for changes in grain farming. He promoted using horses for plowing instead of oxen. Tull developed a mechanical seed drill and a horse-drawn hoe for clearing weeds. Many of Tull's farming ideas helped bring about a revolution in British agriculture.

## Improving the harvest

To harvest the grain, farmers used sickles to cut it in much the same way that early Egyptians did. Eventually harvesters put curved blades, or sickles, on long sticks and created **scythes**. The act of cutting grain with scythes did not change until the mid-1800s. Harvesting grain required many people working many hours. In Europe entire communities worked together to bring in the harvest and then celebrated with a feast, singing, and dancing.

## Rice plantations

One of the first grain crops to come to North America was rice. Although rice originated in Asia, it came to the American colonies from England. South Carolina landowners used plows and **dredges** to change swampland into rice **plantations**. By 1700 rice had become the main crop of South Carolina. The colony shipped rice to England, where the crop brought consistently high prices.

## Threshers

Once the grain was cut, workers used **flails** to beat the grain. Flailing separated the grain from the husk. In 1784 Scottish engineer Andrew Meikle developed a mechanical **thresher**. Meikle's thresher was a major development for grain farming.

Farmers in the 1300s plowed fields much like farmers did 1,000 years earlier.

## McCormick's Reaper

In 1834 Cyrus Hall McCormick developed the **reaper**, which made harvesting easier. Farmers no longer needed a handful of men armed with scythes to cut their wheat crops. The reaper worked like a large, horse-drawn lawn mower.

A McCormick's reaper did the work of six men in less time.

## Mechanizing grain farming

One thing that held back the production of grain was the amount of human work involved in plowing, planting, and harvesting a crop. In 1830 it took about 250 to 300 work hours to produce 100 bushels of wheat, which was the harvest from 5 acres (2 hectares).

By the mid-1800s farmers used steel plows to turn their fields. They used chemical **fertilizers** to increase their crops. Hand power changed to horse power as more farmers owned horses to help them with their work.

## Petroleum power

In 1884 farmers used horse-drawn **combines** to harvest fields of wheat. By 1890 producing 100 bushels of wheat needed only 40 to 50 work hours. The next advance in farming technology was gas-powered equipment. This advance came in 1892, when John Froelich built the first gasoline-powered tractor.

By 1965 it only took about 5 work hours to raise 100 bushels of wheat. By this time, one farmer could grow enough grain, whether it was wheat, corn, barley, oats, or millet, to feed about 25 people for a year. Grain farming advanced far beyond hand plows and sickles.

### John Froelich (1849–1933)

John Froelich was an inventor born in Clayton County, Iowa. He attended school at the College of Iowa, where he became interested in building gas-powered engines. In 1892 he produced a tractor with a 16-horsepower (12-kilowatt) engine. Froelich, a lifelong inventor, also developed a washing machine, a dishwasher and dryer, and a mechanical corn picker.

### Mechanical Picker

Reapers did not work for picking corn. In 1880 Patrick Lawler drew up plans for a mechanical picker. Lawler built his corn picker, which poured out ears of husked corn. No one would buy them. Today, however, most corn farmers use mechanical corn pickers.

# What Exactly Is Grain?

Scientists define grain as the seed of a grass-like plant. This includes wheat, rice, corn, barley, and oats. These plants are types of grass, although they do not look like the grass in a lawn. There are hundreds of **species** of grass, and all of them flower and produce seeds.

**Nutritionists** would say that most seeds that are used whole as food or ground into flour are grain. **Amaranth**, **quinoa**, and buckwheat do not come from grass-like plants. They do produce seeds, and the seeds look like, taste like, and are used like grains. They are sold as grains in stores and ground into flour for breads and cakes just like wheat or corn.

A wheat plant is shown here with its kernels.

## Whole grains or processed grains

Whole grains are the entire **kernel** or seed of grain. The outside, protective coating of the seed remains intact. The seeds can be eaten whole, such as with brown rice. They can be ground into flour, such as with whole wheat flour. Generally, whole grain products have more protein, vitamins, and minerals than those made with **processed** grains.

Most of the **nutrients** in grain are found in the bran, which is the outer covering of grain seeds. Processed grains, such as white rice, remove the bran and lose much of their nutritional value. Brown rice is a whole-grain product. White rice is brown rice that has been milled to get rid of the outer rice coating, called bran.

Some flour, such as white wheat flour used for bread or cakes, is **enriched**. Enriching flour returns some of the nutrients lost from processing. Enriched white flour usually has thiamin, riboflavin, niacin, folic acid, iron, and calcium added to it.

| Percent of daily nutritional value per serving (1 cup/174 grams) | Brown Rice | White Rice |
|---|---|---|
| Carbohydrate | 15% | 12% |
| Fiber | 14% | 7% |
| Protein | 5% | 4% |
| Iron | 6% | 1% |
| Calcium | 2% | 0% |
| Niacin | 13% | 3% |
| Vitamin B6 | 15% | 2% |
| Manganese | 107% | 23% |
| Potassium | 4% | 0% |

Brown rice provides more protein. vitamins. and minerals than white rice.

Definitely not a grass. buckwheat is actually related to rhubarb.

# What Are Some Other Types of Grain?

There are many grains that are not as popular as wheat, rice, or corn. Some of these grains grow in many regions, such as barley and oats. Some grains grow mostly in their native region, such as **quinoa** from Peru and teff from Ethiopia.

Barley was a wild grain collected by **hunter-gatherers**. By 8000 BCE barley was planted and grown as a crop in Mesopotamia, an area now known as Iraq and Syria. People ate barley as a breakfast cereal that was cooked like oatmeal. Today barley mainly feeds animals and is used to make beer. While barley is easy to grow, it is hard to separate barley **groats** from the plant stalks.

## Oats

Today oats are extremely popular in many places around the world. Like most other grains, oats were the seeds of wild-growing grass. They were often found as weeds in early Egyptian wheat fields. The earliest evidence of oat grains were found in Egypt and date to about 2000 BCE. Evidence of farmed oats has also been found in caves in Switzerland.

People eat oats in oatmeal, muffins, cookies, and granola bars. Oats are highly nutritious. Eating oats is known to reduce **cholesterol** in human blood. The grain helps control blood pressure and can reduce the chance of getting cancer. When added to bath water, oats can soothe itchy chicken pox, **eczema**, and sunburn. Oats are also used as cattle and horse feed.

The whitish grain in this soup is barley.

# Rye

Long seen as a weed growing among wheat crops, rye eventually became a farmed grain in cold, northern **climates**. Rye also grows well in high, dry desert areas. It is a traditional grain used for bread and making alcohol in the United States, Canada, Northern Europe, and Russia.

Rye is unusual among grains for its high fiber content. Fiber is important for a healthy digestive system. With most grains the human body converts the grain starches to sugars for energy. Rye does not produce as much blood sugar as other grains, such as wheat or corn. This makes rye especially healthy for **diabetics**, who must limit their sugar intake.

Rye bread usually contains a mix of rye and wheat flours.

Millet makes good cattle feed, which is important in places where there is no grass for grazing.

## Millet

For thousands of years, millet grew wild in Africa and Asia. The grass grows about 5 to 10 feet (1.5 to 3 meters) tall and looks like thin corn stalks. Millet needs little rain and will grow where wheat and barley will not. It is an ideal crop for regions with poor soil, little rainfall, and high temperatures.

Scientists believe that hunter-gatherers ate wild millet more than 10,000 years ago. As with wheat, people began collecting the seeds first, and they did not begin to plant millet as a farm crop until about 4500 BCE in China. In Sudan millet was first farmed about 4000 BCE. The grain is used to make beer or eaten as a hot breakfast cereal. Millet can also be added to soups, stews, or vegetable dishes. It provides protein, B vitamins, calcium, iron, and potassium.

Quinoa comes in many colors,
including white (shown here),
purple, red, and black.

## Buckwheat

Most people think of buckwheat as the ideal flour for pancakes. Japan's soba noodles, France's galettes, and Russia's kasha are all made from buckwheat. Buckwheat seeds, called groats, provide a rich, nutty flavor to foods.

Buckwheat can grow in rocky regions where it is hard to raise wheat or corn. It is not a true grass or a grain, but the groats are so "grain-like" that buckwheat is generally considered a type of grain. Buckwheat is eaten fresh and raw or dried and ground into flour. It thickens soups or gravies or is baked into flatbread. Pillows and furniture filled with buckwheat hulls are popular for people who are **allergic** to feathers.

## Quinoa

Quinoa is pronounced *keen-wah*. The Incas raised quinoa high in the Andes Mountains of South America. The seeds have been collected and **processed** since about 1200 CE. Like buckwheat, quinoa is not technically a grass or a grain. It is generally considered to be a grain because it is eaten as seeds or in flour form. Quinoa seeds are small and look much like sesame seeds. They come in tan, red, purple, and black. Most quinoa still comes from the Andes, but the plants also grow well in the Rocky Mountains of North America.

Quinoa is added to soups, baked goods, and salads. The ground flour is often added to breakfast cereal flakes. Quinoa provides protein, magnesium, and fiber in diets. Because it has no **gluten**, quinoa is good for people on gluten-free diets.

# Why Are Ancient Grains Making a Comeback?

Ancient grains sound like something taken from Egyptian tombs, but they are eaten every day. Most ancient grains are sold in the health food aisle of supermarkets. The grains are also found in modern, whole-grain breads. Ancient grains include spelt, **amaranth**, **quinoa**, teff, **farro**, and kamut.

What makes a grain ancient as opposed to modern? Ancient grains have not changed for thousands of years. Compare amaranth to corn. Amaranth grown today grows, looks, and tastes like amaranth grown 2,000 years ago. Today's corn has been bred to produce neat, tidy rows of yellow or white **kernels**. It looks nothing like the corn the Aztecs grew 1,000 years ago. The corn Aztecs ate had blue, purple, red, and yellow kernels. Once the kernels were dried and ground, Aztec cornmeal was a shade of dark blue.

## High food value

Ancient grains are prized for the food value they provide. Most offer high amounts of protein and fiber. For people with **gluten** allergies, quinoa, amaranth, and spelt have low gluten content. Yet these grains contain all the vitamins and minerals needed for good nutrition. Ancient grains have become part of a health food revolution.

This crop of amaranth provides protein, minerals, and vitamins for a community in Guatemala.

# How Do We Use Grain?

It is obvious that grain is used for food. We feed cattle, dairy cows, poultry, and other livestock on grain, so, indirectly, our meat, poultry, and dairy products also come from grain. Wheat or corn is eaten, in one form or another, at nearly every meal in developed countries. For 60 percent of the world, rice appears on the table daily. What most people do not know is that there are hundreds of uses for grain that do not include food. One advantage of using grains to make nonfood products, such as plastics or oils, is that grains are **renewable**. Farmers can grow more grain.

This lovely red parasol is made from rice paper.

People who have plenty of rice have found clever ways to use this grain. Rice makes excellent animal food and is often put in dog and cat food. Rice straw—the dried stalks—make a good base for growing mushrooms. The straw also makes strong paper, which can be used in printing and as a food. The starchy nature of rice lends itself to being the base of rice glue, which is essential for Japanese paper crafts.

## Working with wheat

Wheat consists of the straw-like stalks and berries, or grain. All parts of wheat plants are used in making a wide variety of products. Because wheat is a high-protein grain, it makes good feed for farmed fish and for turkeys. The grain absorbs water and is often an ingredient in kitty litter. Wheat is also used to make biodegradable plastics, such as coffee cups and plastic forks and spoons.

One common characteristic of wheat is that it contains **gluten**. Some people are **allergic** to gluten, so they must watch what they eat. They also need to watch out for which cosmetics they use. Wheat or wheat gluten is found in face creams, shampoos and conditioners, lipstick, foundation makeup, and powder.

## The most useful grain: corn

A full list of all the uses for corn would take pages. Corn, corn oil, cornstarch, and corn syrup are used to make hundreds of food products, from tortilla shells to chicken gravy to lemonade. There is even corn in chewing gum. Scientists use corn in many surprising ways, including in **ethanol**, which is a common ingredient in car fuel.

Crayons actually contain corn!

In an average day, people come into contact with dozens of corn products without even knowing it. Shaving cream and disposable diapers contain corn products. The crayons children color with and the latex paint on kitchen walls also have corn in them. Corn is in wallpaper and the glue that sticks wallpaper to the walls. It is also in **antibiotics**, such as penicillin, and aspirin.

Like wheat, corn is used in many types of personal products. Many face creams, shampoos and conditioners, and deodorants use a chemical that comes from corn oil. Corn-based chemicals are also found in face powder, blush, lipstick, and mascara.

Corn is also used in some unusual products. Few people would expect that corn is used in manufacturing spark plugs or batteries. Corn is part of the process that makes fireworks. Even the insulation that keeps homes warm depends in part on corn.

### James Caleb Jackson (1811–1895)

James Caleb Jackson invented the first dry, whole-grain breakfast cereal. Jackson worked at a health care facility in Dansville, New York. He believed that diet was an important part of good health. In 1863 he developed Granula, a breakfast cereal made from whole-wheat flour called Graham flour.

# How Does Grain Get from the Field to the Market?

Grain ripens in the field, and then it is harvest time. In many countries, farmers drive huge **combines** in neat rows through the crops. Combines **harvest** grain crops quickly, leaving an empty field behind.

In some countries, grain is still harvested by hand. Workers cut the grain with **scythes** or use **reapers** drawn by horses, mules, or oxen. Other workers **thresh** the grain. Workers collect the stalks, which may be used to feed cattle or to stuff bedding. The grain must also be cleaned. This process, called **winnowing**, separates the usable grain from the husks, called **chaff**. Bringing in the harvest is hard, backbreaking work.

Heavy millet grain falls to the ground, while lighter husks blow away.

A combine cuts and threshes grain in one quick process.

## Storing grain

On a modern farm, grain that is kept for cattle feed is stored in silos. Grain being sent to market is loaded onto trucks or railcars and transported. The grain may be put into sacks for transporting, or it may be shipped in bulk. With bulk shipping, loose grain fills a large container. The container protects the grain from rain or wind.

## Combine Harvester

Combine harvesters, or simply combines, take much of the work out of harvesting grain crops. The machines do three jobs at one time. They reap the harvest. They thresh the grain, separating grain from husks. And they clean the crop. Combines are used to harvest wheat, oats, and rye.

## At the mill

Grain used as food for people is packaged for sale in markets. The grain may need to be washed to get rid of dirt, plant remains, or insects. Some grain is sold as whole grain, and some is sold as flour.

Breakfast cereal manufacturers, commercial bakeries, and pet food companies may buy whole grains by the truckload. These companies may grind the grain themselves. The grain may also go to a mill to be **processed**. The mill packages flour or processed grains for sale in supermarkets and for use by manufacturers.

This rice mill removes the bran from brown rice, producing white rice.

## More than just bread

Wheat and rye flour are commonly found in bread. Cornmeal is also used in baking, as are oats, sorghum, and buckwheat. Pasta, noodles, rice products, baked desserts, and breakfast cereals line the aisles of supermarkets. They are all obvious grain products.

Some less obvious grain products include soda, dog and cat food, and snack foods. Corn syrup is an ingredient in candy bars and ketchup. Oats are one of the main ingredients in granola bars. Grain products provide ingredients used to make some yogurts and dessert toppings. Corn syrup appears in pickles, jams, jellies, salad dressings, and even spaghetti sauce. A look at the ingredients in many grocery items shows a surprising number of grain products in common foods.

A kernel of corn goes through many processes and travels a long way before ending up in many items you buy at the store.

# Can Science Produce More Grain?

**Biotechnology** is using living organisms to make or manufacture something people want to use. It includes the study of ways to make plants or animals grow bigger, produce more crops, or resist disease. In nature stronger, hardier plants thrive. Some people worry about new **species** developed by scientists, particularly when it involves **genetic engineering**. But many scientists state biotechnology is really just working with nature's process of natural selection in laboratories.

For many years, developing countries have been unable to feed their people. Poor soil, **drought**, insects, and plant diseases resulted in poor crops. The **green revolution** uses science to develop grain species that survive in poor conditions. Scientists find ways to help developing nations feed themselves by making grains that succeed where other crops fail. The green revolution has produced wheat that thrives in Mexican deserts and high Indian plains. It has produced high-yield rice and larger ears of corn.

## Norman Borlaug (1914–2009)

Dr. Norman Borlaug, a plant scientist from Iowa, developed a form of short-stalk, high-yield wheat. His efforts won him the Nobel Peace Prize in 1970 for engineering wheat that would help feed the world. Borlaug is considered the founder of the green revolution. He also founded the World Food Prize in 1986 to recognize scientists that contribute to the world food supply.

## Farming in labs

It might seem that wheat is wheat and rice is rice. That is not so. Different species of wheat, for example, grow better in one **climate** than another. They yield more wheat berries and have different food values. Hard red spring wheat has more protein than soft red winter wheat. Durum wheat contains more niacin than hard white wheat. In all there are several hundred varieties of wheat seeds, and nearly all wheat seeds are **hybrids**.

When developing a hybrid, scientists try to grow a new generation of plants with the best characteristics from two other plants. For example, one type of wheat grows well in dry areas. Another type resists plant diseases. Scientists try to produce a new wheat variety that has both of these characteristics. This process is called **selective breeding**.

The green revolution helped India become a world-class grain producer.

## Genetically engineered grain

We have been eating **genetically modified** (GM) grains for years. Nearly all wheat, rice, and corn are hybrids of grains grown hundreds of years ago. Aztec corn featured uneven yellow, blue, and purple **kernels**. The tidy, pale yellow corn we eat today is a hybrid of Aztec corn.

Here are three ways scientists have developed "better" rice. The world's rice is not enough to feed everyone who would normally eat rice. Scientists developed high-yield rice that increased rice crops by 15 to 20 percent. A newly developed "super rice" delivers three times the crop of normal rice. Golden rice, another product of lab science, has more vitamin A than normal rice. In diets that lack vitamin A, golden rice fills that gap.

This type of hybrid rice produces 30 percent more rice per plant than normal rice plants.

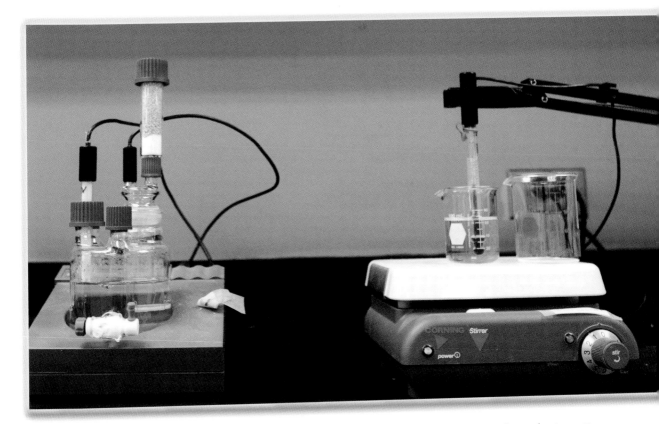

Ethanol is fuel made from corn or other plant matter.

## Grain into fuel

Another area in which biotechnology has made great changes is the production of **ethanol**. Used since the 1820s, ethanol was the fuel Henry Ford used to power his first automobile. The value of biofuel is that it may take the place of petroleum products. Petroleum is not a **renewable** resource, but the grains used to produce biofuel can be grown and **processed** in many places. Ethanol is a corn-based product. Biodiesel may be made from a variety of different seed oils.

# Who Buys and Sells Grain?

Throughout the world the success of grain depends on several factors. Grain needs sun, good soil, and water. Too much water or **drought** conditions destroy crops. Natural disasters such as hurricanes, floods, insects, and plant diseases destroy grain crops. The loss of a crop affects human diets by reducing the amount of grain we eat. Loss of grain crops also affects our protein sources. Beef cattle, poultry, farmed fish, hogs, and sheep eat grains. The loss of grains will reduce the amount of meat, chicken, or fish available and increase the cost of that food.

## Case study: Australia's drought

Over the past decade, Australia's major grain-producing region has suffered drought. Australian rice crops are down to 2 percent of what they were 10 years ago. Once, Australia sold extra rice. Today the country needs to import rice. Wheat crops are nearly as bad. Australia normally grows 15 percent of the world's wheat. When wheat crops fail, farmers lose their farms and the country's economy suffers.

This Australian wheat crop is stunted from drought and produces much less grain than Australia needs.

## Changing wheat production

Wheat production has changed. India and China now grow more wheat than the United States or Russia. The developing world's share of wheat production is about 60 percent of the total world crop. Major wheat users in Asia include China, India, Iran, Pakistan, and Turkey.

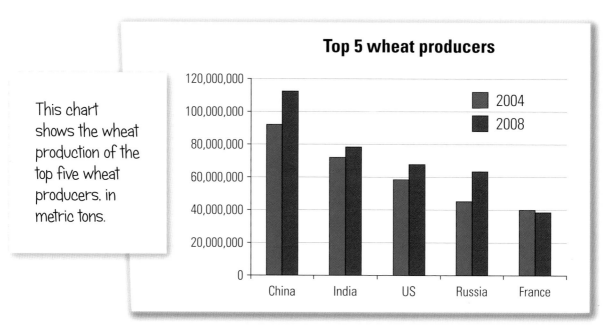

This chart shows the wheat production of the top five wheat producers, in metric tons.

## Rice production

According to the United Nations Food and Agriculture Organization (FAO), 93.3 percent of the world's rice production comes from seven countries. China and India grow the most rice. They also eat most of the rice they grow. Japan, a major rice consumer, is facing a serious rice shortage. Japan can no longer grow enough rice to feed its people. In 2011 Japan suffered an earthquake and tsunami. The tsunami deposited salt in the soil of the Tohoku region of northern Japan. Tohoku grows 26 percent of Japan's rice. In recent years Japan has imported 660,000 tons (600,000 metric tons) of rice a year. If the rice fields of Tohoku fail, Japan will need to import even more rice.

## Other grains

The European Union and Russia are the world's largest producers of barley, rye, and oats. Russia, Canada, and Ukraine use the most barley. Rye is one of the few grains that can be used in making yeast bread. Northern European countries, such as Belarus, Poland, and Germany, use large amounts of rye, but Russia is the largest consumer of this grain. Oats are commonly used to feed cattle and horses or as hot breakfast cereal. Russia, the United States, and Canada use the most oats.

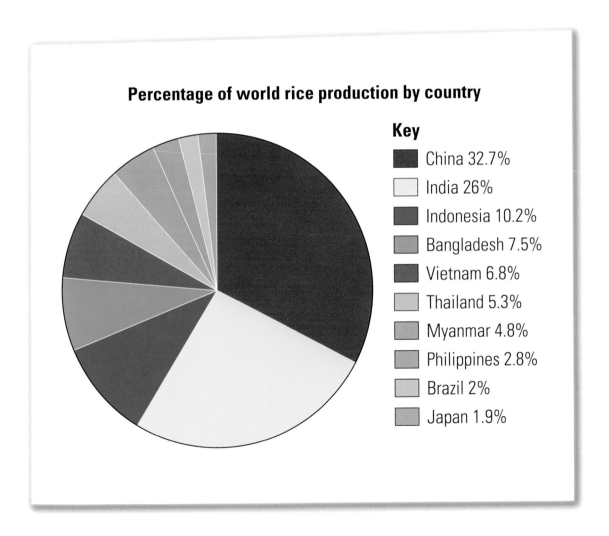

**Percentage of world rice production by country**

**Key**
- China 32.7%
- India 26%
- Indonesia 10.2%
- Bangladesh 7.5%
- Vietnam 6.8%
- Thailand 5.3%
- Myanmar 4.8%
- Philippines 2.8%
- Brazil 2%
- Japan 1.9%

# Can Grains End World Hunger?

Despite the ability of some nations to produce large quantities of grain, the world does not grow enough grain to feed everyone. **Drought**, war, and disease leave millions of people unfed or underfed. Grains are important in the fight against hunger. They provide nutrition and energy and are fairly inexpensive. A bowl of brown rice costs only pennies compared to the price of chicken or beef.

Relief agencies such as the United Nations World Food Program try to feed those without enough food in several ways. They ship grain to regions where hungry people live. It is not easy to ensure the grain reaches those who need it. Agencies work with farmers to help the hungry feed themselves. They help dig wells and provide quality seed for growing grains.

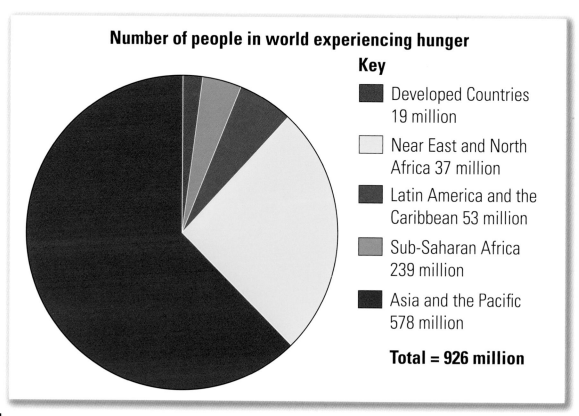

**Number of people in world experiencing hunger**

**Key**

■ Developed Countries 19 million

□ Near East and North Africa 37 million

■ Latin America and the Caribbean 53 million

■ Sub-Saharan Africa 239 million

■ Asia and the Pacific 578 million

**Total = 926 million**

In 2011 more than half of people without enough food in the world lived in Asia.

## People causing hunger

While it is easy to blame nature for crop failure, humans also cause hunger. War destroys crops, displaces people, and leaves many people with no way to feed themselves. Greed also gets its share of blame. Too often grain sent to relieve hunger is stolen and sold by people in power.

## The cycle of hunger

Turning barren land into grain crops is not quick or easy. In many places, farmers do not have modern technology to plow, seed, or water their fields. They **harvest** and process grain by hand. Poor seed planted in worn-out soil produces low-yield crops. The solution to this problem is educating farmers on better ways of growing grain. That step includes providing tractors and harvesters. It also depends on seed that will grow drought-resistant, high-yield grain.

### Gebisa Ejeta
### (born 1950)

One of Africa's biggest problems is growing grain in drought-ridden areas. Ethiopian Gebisa Ejeta bred a **hybrid** type of sorghum that grows with very little water. Sorghum is usually eaten as porridge or fed to livestock. Ejeta won the World Food Prize in 2009 for his work in developing hardy types of sorghum to feed the hungry in Ethiopia and Sudan.

## Robotic Rice Planter

Robotic rice planters can plant a rice paddy in far less time and more efficiently than humans. Cutting down on human labor and planting more productive types of rice will increase rice crops. Asian people depend on rice as a **staple** in their diets. Rice planters can help feed Asia's hungry.

A robotic rice planter takes the labor out of planting rice in Japan.

This wheat is ready for harvest.

## The solution

The solution to hunger is to teach **sustainable** grain farming. Sustainable grain farming means taking advantage of every plot of usable soil. It means conserving soil and water. Sustainable farming requires proper grain storage that reduces grain loss. In recent years, nearly 40 percent of grain harvested in developing countries rotted in poor storage facilities. Distributing grain is an issue that needs improvement. For example in 2010, 50,000 tons (45,000 metric tons) of wheat in India sat in railroad cars and spoiled. India has too many hungry people to have this kind of waste.

High-yield, productive grain seed can produce more grain, but seed is only one aspect of a very large problem. There is no quick solution to world hunger. This is a complex issue that includes farming technology, soil quality, **irrigation**, better seed quality, and **fertilizer**. Countries that produce large quantities of grain need to help those that struggle, farm by farm and crop by crop.

# Glossary

**agriculture** job of farming or raising crops

**allergic** having a strong negative reaction to a substance

**amaranth** flowering plant raised for food

**antibiotics** substances that kill bacteria

**biotechnology** use of living things to produce products or improve the environment

**chaff** grain husks

**cholesterol** group of solid fats found in animal blood

**clan** group of related people

**climate** general weather conditions of an area

**combine** machine that reaps, threshes, and cleans grain

**diabetic** person whose body has difficulty using sugars and starches

**dredge** machine used for moving earth

**drought** long period without sufficient rainfall

**eczema** skin problem that causes red, itchy, or scaly skin

**enrich** treat with added protein, vitamins, or minerals

**ethanol** fuel made from plant fibers

**farro** food made with whole-wheat grains

**fertilizer** chemical substance that helps plants grow

**flail** tool used to separate grain from its husks by beating the grain

**genetic engineering** science of changing the genetic makeup of a living thing

**genetically modified** substances that have been changed at their most basic level

**gluten** gluey substance found in wheat or rye flour

**green revolution** scientific effort to help developing countries grow better crops

**groats** hulled kernels of grain

**harvest** collect a crop

**hunter-gatherer** early human who lived by hunting and collecting food but had no fixed home base

**hybrid** offspring of plants produced by crossbreeding two species of the same plant

**irrigation** system of watering plants

**kernel** soft, edible part of grain

**nutrient** substance that sustains life, health, or growth, such as vitamins and minerals

**nutritionist** person trained in determining foods that support life, health, or growth

**plantation** large farm dedicated to one main crop

**plow** tool used to break up soil

**processed** treated or prepared for use

**quinoa** ancient grain-like food of the Incas

**reaper** mechanical grain cutting machine

**renewable** able to be reproduced

**scythe** long-handled cutting tool

**selective breeding** process of developing new types of plants with the best characteristics of parent plants

**sickle** short-handled, curved blade

**species** class of individuals having common characteristics or traits

**staple** basic food of a person's diet

**sustainable** able to last a long time

**thatch** plant material used to cover a roof

**thresh** to separate grain from chaff

**thresher** machine that separates grain from chaff

**winnowing** freeing grain from its husks

# Find Out More

## Books

Lackey, Jennifer D. B. *The Biography of Wheat*. New York: Crabtree, 2007.

Micucci, Charles. *The Life and Times of Corn*. Boston: Houghton Mifflin, 2009.

Raum, Elizabeth. *The Story Behind Bread*. Chicago: Heinemann Library, 2009.

Reynolds, Jan. *Cycle of Rice, Cycle of Life: A Story of Sustainable Farming*. New York: Lee & Low, 2009.

Schaefer, Lola M. *Grains (Food Groups)*. Chicago: Heinemann Library, 2007.

Sertori, Trisha. *Grains, Bread, Cereal, and Pasta*. Tarrytown, N.Y.: Marshall Cavendish, 2008.

Sobol, Richard. *The Life of Rice: From Seedling to Supper*. Somerville, Mass.: Candlewick, 2010.

Sutcliffe, Jane. *John Deere*. Minneapolis, Minn.: Lerner, 2007.

## Websites

### Alternative Grains

You can find out more at this website about alternative grains such as amaranth, kamut, quinoa, millet, spelt, and wild rice.

www.alive.com/2102a5a2.php?subject_bread_cramb=491

### The Great Corn Adventure

The Great Corn Adventure is a complete guide, including narration, for students to learn the history of corn, how corn grows, the stages of corn growth, how corn is harvested, and how corn is used.

http://urbanext.illinois.edu/corn

### History for Kids

Find out when and where people started farming and how it was done in ancient and historic times.

www.historyforkids.org/learn/economy/farming

## History of Wheat

This website discusses the history of wheat. As farming improved, so did the grain. The amount of grain harvested also increased. Find out how wheat became the plant that changed the world.

www.allaboutwheat.info/history.html

## The USA Rice Federation

This USA Rice Federation website is your source for rice information, including rice recipes, preparation instructions, and storage tips.

www.usarice.com

## The Wheat Foods Council

The Wheat Foods Council wants to promote the consumption of grain. This website provides nutrition information, recipes, and lists of food for wheat, fiber, grains, whole wheat, and whole grains.

www.wheatfoods.org

# Places to visit

## The Farmers' Museum

5775 State Highway 80
Cooperstown, NY 13326
607-547-1450
The Farmers' Museum in New York state is one of the oldest rural (country) life museums in the United States.

www.farmersmuseum.org

## The Mennonite Heritage and Agricultural Museum

200 N. Poplar
Goessel, KS 67053
620-367-8200
Mennonites came to Kansas from Russia in 1874 and brought Turkey Red wheat with them to plant on their farms.

www.skyways.org/museums/goessel/index.html

# Index